The Secrets to a Happy Marriage of Nearly Half a Century–and Beyond

(It Is As Strong As the First Day)

by Terry Ring Schonwald and Avi Schonwald

Dorrance Publishing Co
585 Alpha Drive
Suite 103
Pittsburgh, PA 15238
Visit our website at *www.dorrancebookstore.com*

ISBN: 979-8-88812-112-2
eISBN: 979-8-88812-612-7

The Secrets to a Happy Marriage of Nearly Half a Century—and Beyond

(It is as strong as the first day)

CONTENTS

ACKNOWLEDGMENTS

Avi's parents shared their loving experiences with him and he often brings up just how his father loved his mother!

Terry's parents also shared the loving experiences with her and her father often commented on how lucky he was that his lovely girlfriend actually married him!

INTRODUCTION

Before you tie the knot, sit down with each other and talk about what you want.

Do you see children in your future? How many do you want? Does he also want children? How many?

I knew what kind of a heart my "boyfriend" had when we had that talk. He said, "If it would harm one hair on your head to get pregnant, we'll adopt."

He also showed his goodness, when he had a small job and he had someone helping him. I said I could have helped him with that. He said, "My dear, my friend needs the money and if I give him the money and he can't pay me back—I lose a friend! If he works for the money, he feels good about himself—and I keep a friend!"

Those two conversations, let me know what kindness he showed to everyone and how endearing that was.

We got married in 1979. We said our I-dos and meant it, so how were we going to last when others were divorcing each other all around us!

Another thing I noticed is both of us treat people respectfully no matter who or where, always a thank-you! We see people as we see apples. Apples come in red, green, and yellow and they are all apples! People come in red, brown, black, and white and they are all people! We both learned this lesson from our parents and we live by it! We taught our kids to do the same.

We keep each other in mind. For example, English is my husband's fourth language and he wasn't schooled in it, so when he needs a word spelled correctly, he asks me and pays me with a kiss!

We are big on payments with a kiss or two or three!

By the way, neither of us leave the house when the other is left inside, without a kiss goodbye and then a kiss hello when we return. It has been like that for the past forty-four years!

"Where is home my love?"

He answers. "In between your arms!"

We celebrate everything.

No two people ever always see the same thing the same way. Agree to disagree and don't go to bed mad at each other.

If you are not sure that you heard correctly, ask the other person to say again what the comment was. Don't expect the other person to understand your meaning exactly, because everyone "hears" through their mind full of what came before you! If one of you is using hearing aids, the other person should face that person so there is no question of what you said! If it is something requiring doing something, verify that your significant other understood what you said.

When we were newly married, we called each other "my love" and we still do, nearly half a century later! It was true then and even a stronger meaning now.

CHAPTER 1
Getting to know each other

Learn about each other. Have fun with each other. After you know each other for a few dates, if you think this is going to be your future mate, it is time for a serious conversation. First, what is your idea of a family? For some people, having a dog or cat fulfills their idea of a family. If kids are your idea of a complete family—how many? What is the other person's idea of a family? And if kids, how many? If you are not in agreement at this point, your chances of a successful, loving relationship is not starting on solid ground.

If you both agree you want children, and you agreed about the number of them, what happens if one of you is not fertile and cannot have kids? Do you both agree on a surrogate or In-vitro fertilization? If these two methods are not available, do you both agree on adoption?

These basic questions are the foundation for a solid, healthy relationship.

Sex may be wonderful, but that is not the only criteria or foundation for a lasting, happy marriage. Sex is only one of the ways you'll enjoy married life. Sex and caring for each other should be an expression of love for each other. Sex becomes love making!

Learn how to give a good massage! It will release a lot of tension!

A wise man (my husband's father) said that three words were the basis for a good, joyful, sexual relationship—COMMUNICATION (1), COMMUNICATION (2), COMMUNICATION (3).

COMMUNICATION #1 - You tell your significant other, what you don't like—whether it is verbal or physical. There is nothing more annoying than your partner doing something irritating that you just can't tolerate while he thinks that because it worked for someone else, you must like it too! Apparently, you didn't communicate with each other, what annoys you. A small example is a kiss on the ear. For many it is very sensual, but for some people it can be torture! No one is a mind reader—speak up.

COMMUNICATION #2 - You tell your significant other, what you do like—whether it is verbal or physical. If you have a nickname that you love to hear or any area on your body that you love to be kissed, as an example, let your partner know. If there is anything else you like, let your partner know. This way you both will have a joyful relationship that you can look forward to. For both Communication 1 and 2 use these skills in your day to day lives and you will have a wonderful life together.

COMMUNICATION #3 – Don't take your partner for granted. It can destroy even the most solid relationship, for example, your friend from out of town arrived and you want to have dinner with him. Ask your spouse if he/she cooked dinner for that evening? If so, can we have a guest for dinner? You don't know what he/she planned, because you didn't ask! Maybe he/she had a surprise for you with tickets to your favorite ballgame or a hot, sexy date planned! Before you give an answer to your out-of-town friend, talk with your partner. He/she will appreciate the fact that they are not taken for granted.

A person can change their clothing many times a day, but they are still the same person! Behavior and your attitude will speak volumes about you; more than any clothes or jewelry that you can put on. That fact does not change regardless of the years you are together. Feelings for each other should get stronger through the years and the desire for each other should grow stronger with time, like good wine.

Be certain to let your partner know what is important to you in life.

Are charities an important topic in your life? Are you willing to support them financially or personally?

Are human rights important to you and yours? Are you willing to take a stand for your position? Is your partner willing to take a stand as well?

If he/she is not in agreement with you, are you willing to accept and live with that? There are times in life that human rights are trampled on. This subject can take a serious turn in your relationship. If you don't know about it in advance, it could be a negative discovery between the two of you. For some people, it would be a heavy negative point about you.

How important is higher education to each of you, in regards to your children: If you both agree on higher education how will you provide for it?

Some parents don't plan ahead for higher education, and their children end up with student loans for years to come! Not paying on time can affect their credit score for many years more.

Before we get to higher education, let's talk about who is going to raise our kids. If you both agree that you want children and you are both working out of the house—who will raise your kids? Think about what kind of work one of you might do from home that will help pay the bills. That way, one of you is always in sight of your offspring. This way, the kids won't ever have a parentless home. In some cases, grandparents might provide the environment that lets both parents work outside. This situation might work when the grandparents live with you.

By the way, when a woman is pregnant, it is quite possible to be more swollen in your ninth month than all the other eight put together.

CHAPTER 2
Dating all through your lives together

Act like every "date" is the first date. If you do, you will never get tired of each other.

I dress for myself and for my husband. I will ask him, "PRESENTABLE?" If he says, I want to peel them off of you, I know I have dressed for him presentably! If he doesn't say that, I probably will change my clothes to suit his taste. Afterall, when we are walking together, he likes to see me presentably!

I always go clothes shopping with him, because he always tells me the truth—"Does it look better on me, or on the hanger?"

We hold hands when we get out of the car until we reach our destination. And if we can, we always try to sit next to each other.

My husband often tells me, as he did decades ago, that Home is between your arms. I never get tired of hearing that from him!

And sometimes we call each other to say, "I just called to say I love you!" Some people we know set a day of the week and date each other. We just date each other, no matter what day it is!

We always have each other's back.

My husband is deathly allergic to fish oil and that is something I have watched out for as soon as he mentioned it to me.

He doesn't like roasted turkey, so I will cook the turkey on Thanksgiving, but also cook a beef brisket and potatoes, because he loves that! I want to make him happy. I look for ways to make him happy and he does the same for me.

I often tell him, "I can't eat certain things when you're not home." As it turns out, jars are often impossible for me to open. When he puts his strong hands on the jar they open immediately, as if he said "open sesame" and they open!

Thank you!—I think those words are spoken almost as often as *I love you!*

We thank our children, the mail carriers, delivery people, our neighbors, whoever does something on our behalf. Everyone wants to know that they are not being taken for granted and Thank you is always returned with a smile. If we can make someone's day better with a thank-you, we would say it all day!

CHAPTER 3
Be a role model for your kids

Don't hesitate to show affection for each other in front of the kids. They learn by example. The way you treat each other will be a roadmap for your children's future relationships.

We greet each other with a hug and a kiss, leaving and coming home whether or not the kids are in the room.

It is very important to support your children's choices. Kids remember throughout their lives how you supported them and dealt with each other. That helps build their character.

When the kids get older, it is important to explain to them how you reach a conclusion and any decision that you do, as an age-appropriate subject.

We decided that it was important for us to show our physical presence at their chosen activities. When we were involved in our children's activities, many of the other kids came to us to ask why their parents weren't there to watch them or participate like we did?

When one of our children's friends, who knew I knew him, from the extra curriculum activities, needed a recommendation letter for the Marines, he came to me to write the letter. We knew that child for years and years and we provided him with the needed recommendation letter. He successfully joined the Marines and today has a wonderful family of his own. The same young man often asked questions of my husband, since his absent father couldn't provide them for him.

CHAPTER 4
Public Displays of Affection

When you are out and about, holding hands should not stop after you are married, because you are still boyfriend and girlfriend for the rest of your life, if you are lucky to understand the importance of it. Just because you got married you should not stop showing affection for each other. We hold hands as we walk down the street and people ask us are we newlyweds? We answer yes for the last forty-three years! Why is it such a surprise to people that we still hold hands after forty-three years? Those who don't hold hands are taking their relationship for granted and they are not displaying their closeness and feelings for each other to their kids. Kids will follow their parents' behavior and example. If you don't give them the signs that you care for each other, they will emulate you in their relationships. Be open to your kids and clarify for them how important relationships are and when you get upset with the other one, it doesn't mean you stop loving each other, because you have agreed to disagree.

Often, my husband will introduce me as his girlfriend and then the question back to him is: "Does your wife know?" His answer is "This is my wife! She's still my girl-friend!" The surprise on people's faces tells us how important strong relationships are. Our relationship has gotten stronger and stronger as we age.

Giving your spouse flowers or candy from time to time will show your children the appreciation for each other. Our adult daughter always brings us flowers almost every time she walks through the door and our adult son surprises us from time to time with delicious meals that he has cooked. YUM YUM! Both of them have very busy schedules, but find time to do something special for us!

BE CHARITABLE

Pick a charity that is close to your heart and when you can, provide them with what you can.

You and your spouse came from different places, and placement in your varying families. So, you may think differently about various topics. Agree to disagree.

Never bring a disagreement into your bedroom. And keep a television out of the bedroom so you won't have to agree to disagree. The bedroom is a sacred place for sleeping and making love and protecting the relationship.

A good warm hug and a kiss and a great back rub can dissolve many disagreements before they become an issue.

In this computer age, anyone can do research on any topic. But when it comes to the subject of the heart, the computer cannot solve the questions of why we like or dislike certain things.

Agree to disagree, because no two people ever agree on every subject.

The importance of feelings in a family could be a point of disagreement, when a certain other person that one spouse likes and the other doesn't share that opinion of the other person, you have to agree to disagree.

CHAPTER 5
FEELINGS

You owe it to yourself to enjoy life as best you can, while you can. Remember, a day that passes by cannot be retrieved. Only memories you made that day can be retrieved and shared.

When you see an attractive person on the street, you can appreciate that look or appearance of that person. But appreciation to each other's appearance has a much deeper value in your life. It is important to keep ourselves in good shape, to keep the attraction to each other.

Some people have unreasonable expectations of their significant other. A woman, after her pregnancy will look different than before her pregnant body.

Please accept the fact that as we age, some age more gracefully than others. A good regimen of exercise can help.

One way of maintaining your strength and physical appearance is a good vitamin regimen. And for women, after menopause continued natural hormone therapy will keep your sexuality viable and your youthful appearance. Some people think having an orange or an apple a day, will do the job, however the truth is to have enough Vitamin C to prevent oxidation, which is the main purpose of taking Vitamin C, you would need a dozen oranges every day! A couple of 1000mg tablets of Vitamin C did the job for us and did not upset our stomachs! This is one example of a very important vitamin that will keep you healthy. And the older you get, the more important vitamins become. Another example is Vitamin E, which helps keep your hair on your head and your skin young-looking and viable. It also helps your eyesight. Vitamins helps maintain your entire body's functions. My husband and I don't get sick, even when we are around people who are sick.

Celebrations of events in your lives is a very important part of your life and it is a good way to appreciate life. Every anniversary just adds more value to your relationship. We celebrate every anniversary and the big anniversary dates are celebrated with friends and family members!

Even small events can build memories and the more memories you have, the better life is.

CHAPTER 6
Your Advanced Health Wishes and a Trust

If you have the opportunity to make a trust for yourselves and your advanced health wishes are known, put them into your Will. Also, if you have the ability to pay for your gravesites, do so. This will eliminate the need for your children to make difficult decisions when they are mourning. We took care of both the Advanced Health Wishes and our Trust and then we purchased our gravesites and let our children know the details in written form.

CHAPTER 7
Building Positive Memories

When you have the opportunity to take a vacation with your children, no matter how long or short it may be, and whatever you can afford, it is extremely important to show the reward for your life's work. Everyday life chores should not be taken for granted. A vacation should be a pleasant event with lots of good memories. Take time to vacation. Simple activities that are different from your daily routine will help to build your positive memories. For example, when our children were two and three years old, we traveled by car for a few hours to visit our family in the desert. We stayed with them for a few days. We took the tram (the cable train) to the top of the mountain where there was snow! Our kids got to build a snowman for the first time in their lives!

We took pictures of them and their snowman that they wanted to take home. Several onlookers commented what a fine snowman. We convinced our kids to leave the snowman where everyone at the top of the mountain could see it and they agreed. We made photo albums for each of the kids for their positive memories that they can share with their friends and their families. This was an example of what we did, which fit in our new family budget. While some people can afford to vacation in other countries and elaborate vacations, taking tours is a much less costly option that is planned for you and saves hours and days trying to get reservations of all kinds.

Fit your vacation to your budget! You don't want to be looking at your vacation bill for years to come.

CHAPTER 8
Buying a House

For a young working couple, that has started a family with children, it is important to build for and start the process of buying a home, within their means. It is the biggest investment of their life. A very important detail in this process is to find a home within the boundaries of the school they would like to see their kids in. Some people are looking for a public school, some a magnet school, some a private school, and some are looking for a religious school. How far will you have to drive your children to school, before you drive to work yourself?

With the price of fuel rising in a drastic way, you should consider trading in your gas guzzler for a hybrid or electric car, which will help to clean the environment future for your kids. This is another major expense, but once it is paid for, it will save you the gas money, that could be over $100 a week. Depending on the number of children in your family and how many different schools they attend, it can severely affect your everyday budget, which will affect your ability to buy and maintain a house.

Buying a house for most people is a lifelong financial commitment. Be sure you check with the local authorities on restriction, because some cities have severe restrictions on changing the style of the house in an historical area. In some other areas, there are restrictions on the total square footage of the house and you cannot change that. If you need more room, in that area you will not be able to build on. The restrictions can start at the foundation and end at the roof.

Another point to consider when buying a house is the local parking restrictions. In some areas you cannot park on the street overnight. Some areas restrict the number of cars by marking the parking space on the road.

If you want to run a business from home, there are severe restrictions in some areas that will not allow it.

Our hope is that you all have a successful loving relationship, physically and emotionally. That is the secret of a Happy Marriage for nearly half a century and beyond.